Apollinaire's Speech to the War Medic

Apollinaire's Speech to the War Medic

JAKE KENNEDY

BookThug *MMXI* Toronto

FIRST EDITION
copyright © Jake Kennedy, 2011

The production of this book was made possible through the generous assistance of The Canada Council for The Arts and The Ontario Arts Council.

Printed in Canada

Library and Archives Canada Cataloguing in Publication

Kennedy, Jake, 1972 –
    Apollinaire's speech to the war medic / Jake Kennedy.

Poems.
ISBN 978-1-897388-77-8

    I. Title.

PS8621.E634A66 2011   C811'.6   C2011-901535-8

Table of Contents

Apollinaire's Speech to the War Medic

Light & Char

IN MEMORY OF

George Kennedy
and
Emi Clarke

Apollinaire's Speech to the War Medic

Study of a Claw Hammer

the rearing horse
the samurai's helmet
the photographer under his cape

the opposite of the claw hammer
is the lapsed will,
a yolk that tears itself
on the shell's tooth
and globs outside the pan

there's very little pain
in it, that's why it seeks to know hurt
over and over

one erased face
testing surface, resistance,
and thresholds – these are
ceaseless what am I's
of *bang, bang, bang*

it's an object that doesn't believe at all
in others
or it believes too much

Beckett

Knife

A speech act is when something like a knife enters into the
conversation. A speech act involves speaking to a person
but also putting on a little play. Not just with your arm but
with your voice you can stab someone: that is a speech act
because you are talking and doing simultaneously. A speech
act is a reason to believe that speech is active and that action
is always about speech. Perhaps a speech act is the last act
of speech before silence. When I remember my childhood I
can hardly breathe.

Hole

In this space the words do not meet their destinations. The
words start out alright but they end up turning into other
things. I have seen this happen, but on a different scale: 'We
walked to the' and what comes after the 'the' is a hawk in
the sky. *Appearing to take away our speech.* Essentially these
ideas get silenced, it is sometimes a case of substitutions.
The environment takes over from the talking. In this space,
the knife is leaning over to the lung. The lung is also calling
to the knife. We have tended to characterize violent acts as
unspeakable.

Lung

I have not heard a word. Nothing comes to me here. I
am a blank sidewalk, a clinking street lamp, a runaway
alley can. I've got nothing and hear nothing. I know that
everything I was going to say is wrong and will continue to
be wrong. My philosophy is for shit. My art is for shit. This
really hurts. I am hurt. Do you like this? It seems there is no
division between I-can-speak-to-you and I-can-kill-you. I
can't say I like it. Silence tells the truth of the 'inability of
words' but it doesn't tell the truth about the extent of the
pain.

Study of a Bowl of Squash

"Out of the belly of Christopher's ship a mob bursts"
— Jeannette Armstrong

There are villages on fire
within the ornamentals.

Within the acorns
there are lanterns
coming across the fields.

The butternut predicts museums,
at least marble plinths
on which to set
an exemplar of bounty.

Bounty is the result of
extraction: the squash leaves
the vine as easily as the body
leaves the way of life.

Here are the skulls
in a bowl made of apple wood.

Study of Cat Piss

to have been and
continue to be

maligned: that steeping
becoming the belief

integral to
whatever it meets:

that nothing is truer
than itself

and what are its needs anyway
just to have place

and to be acknowledged
as in total possession of it

from now on

Study of 'Black Snake Pot'
after Carl Beam and borrowing a line from "Deathfugue"

Vessel for Celan's milk.
The cinching cable.

To strangle another's throat
or to hold on with a more meaningful claim?

"There's a man in this house who cultivates snakes."
Because of this fostering, the earth lives?

Despite its assassins!
As if all the shipping containers held medicine.

The mouth of the snake.
The mouth of the pot.

The I that belongs to the hand-built-world;
when an individual wants to use a word (any word) beyond
     irony: i.e., with some responsibility.

Bushestina

Texas is good.
I love the place.
You can barbecue.
You can golf.
I like dogs.
I feel safe.

Do you feel safe?
If so, that's good.
Some folks need dogs
to protect their place.
I like golf.
Do you like barbecues?

I do. I love barbecued
Texas beef — yes, it's safe!
Do you golf?
I do. Golf is pretty good.
I've played all over the place.
Do you have dogs?

Spotty and Barney are my dogs.
They like barbecues.
Once I won second place
in a grill-off. Are dogs safe?
I think so. Dogs are good.
Almost as good as golf.

I said almost! Golf
is better than dogs
because while dogs are good
golf is a bit better. I barbecue
pretty often. I have a big wall safe.
It's in the same place

that Reagan used when this place
was his. Reagan loved golf.
The combo to my wall safe
is ... top secret! I love my dogs.
I love this Weber barbecue.
Are women good?

I think so. A good woman helps you find your place.
I really like barbecues, traveling, and golf.
Do you love dogs? I feel safe.

Sea Study

Why not respect the deadlock in a coral reef?
And, on behalf of impasse, just shut up and wait.

Shut up.
The cars meet each other on city streets and stop.

This too is the sea.
Please shut up.

There are anonymous accumulations of sunlight and water
that are not the sea in the morning.

For instance, crumpled math homework
and bits of windshield on a roadway.

Why not start from belief?
The sand clears itself of furniture.

Two blue whales arrive.
Why not start from holy shit and end there?

And so there is no solution.
And so –

Newly Free Translation
after William Carlos Williams

If 'so' was salt and 'much' was grass and 'depends' was
anchors and 'upon' was time and 'a' was then and 'red' was
crenellated and 'wheel' was frost and 'barrow' was bin and
'glazed' was ambience and 'with' was approximately and
'rain' was yeast and 'water' was wisdom and 'beside' was
streaking and 'the' was that and 'white' was rotunda and
'chickens' was Philadelphia then

salt grass anchors
time
then crenellated frost
bin
ambience approximately yeast
wisdom
streaking that rotunda
Philadelphia
thus allowing the wheelbarrow, the rain water, and the
      chickens to be newly free.

Study of A Subdivision Sidewalk

to know what nothing's about
or to be against all knowing by receiving it

as same: rain, skin, blood, bird droppings,
necklaces, coins, bike tires, chalk, teeth

to be free of causes
and indifferent to flowers, say, or fire

a prison blanket at Vladivostok
a type of tablature

in which all notes have been scoured

The drive-in is Real
for Joanne Gailius

This is the standard blank. On it, the projected hot dogs
are hot dogs and use their many legs to run into the doughy
beds. Are we hungry? Call it a congregation of appetites.
Only one massive wall awaits. Will we be what it wants?
And, what is it when there's nothing yet — not even dusk —
and the shadow-hands are doing rabbit-into-swan? I notice
a diagram of stars, a frame of light that makes a house
around the screen. There are no details within. Then it
shows values, news, money, and the problem of waiting.
It's no use intellectualizing fugitive desire. But let's try.
There are a bunch of pronouns now, flashing. They live
on a screen in the middle of the night. Sometimes they
hate work and there is a leap into the adjacent landscape.
There they are, running over our hot mountains. The faces'
measurements are the greatest for being immeasurable. I
say starlight, starlight into the armored speaker and this is
a form of counter-seduction. So, featured this evening: A
loves B but B is preoccupied with C and C is indifferent to
the entire alphabet. Plus, a creature stirs in a world called
the inevitable. Yep, it's a real doozy. What happens if dust
shows up to symbolize all of these uncontainable anxieties?
Well, we take a break: watch the motes glide in on their
incandescent beam — they drift between the spaces of the
garbage drums. Then back to the restored reflections that go
right into the holes called "very wide expectations": Alex
and Bob, Bob and Carol, or Carol and company all have

a series of receptive openings. They rarely blink. Here we are, ready to admit that there are bounties of pleasure – for everyone. So, the lagoon is not real and the monster is real and the words are not real and the light is real and the hair-dos are not real and the yearning is real. It's no use deciding. A reaches for B. Finally, the universe is simple.

Study of Dog Print in Snow

the sun going down
teeth of the miter saw

explosion
in a prison wall

having been to a place
and needing to go on,

well, do it: exit
despite the bad-ass years

under a crown of shadows
with four drops of rain

falling into the mouth
of the stone well

the spatulate leaves
around the manhole

silhouette of the carnival wheel
before an eclipse

Pallid Sortie, Sure

all human beings are more or less agitated
love sucks goat, by the way

because – who knows?
fire only wants escape from the boredom of wood

logs themselves want a return to stature
according to the up and down breathing of the lake the lake
      is mostly at peace

finally, full of knowledge, there is righteous indifference to
      events and their turns
because – because? because is there ever a moment of utter
      un⁄longing?

paper lanterns that drape the sides of the boat also decorate
      the harbor water
and the boat that turns on the anchor's axis also turns the
      big and little hands of the clock

Study of Rotted Canoe

to witness
a house after the twister

the tugging of the rabbit's clothes
from the rabbit

why 'in need'?
and awaiting what mercy?

screw that pity
for the grin that cannot swallow

stuffed with leaves,
pebbled with rabbit shit

i.e. the bedding-ground
of hollow men

as if there ever was
escape – well, the boat never

promoted it, remaining (still)
an advocate for buoyancy

only indifferent
to romance traditions

History of a Tiger

How should it – jaws locked – explain to the victim a coming-of-age story? First, it uncovers shared fears and draws connections between all communities. Blood appears. The marvel is that normal people really do understand extraordinary suffering. Go on, they say. Yet the tiger never implicates.

There is a 1/1000 probability that the subject or the subject's family will be swallowed whole. Inside, the universe is reportedly a suburban night. Is this improbable? An electronic piano plays. Is this implausible? The moon comes through the eyes and courses down the black hill of the throat. That sliding light is phosphorescent indigo. This tunnel is a history of strange torsions. It is as if the victim's swallowed face is wearing the mask of the tiger, breathing its breath and seeing its sights. The video shows that beyond comradeship eating a stranger offers moments of religious euphoria. At last the human body has discovered the end-point of being a sports fan and begins screaming for itself.

It does not read late into the night. It lives at a sensitive remove from language and its catching inexactitude. Wanting, seeking, and finding, we know, is not a linear enterprise. As the morning rises in the shape of half an eyeball, all beliefs are new. The sunlight offers a version of the way the world used to see itself yesterday – one way of illuminating the future, over and over again. And that is what makes the tiger so sleepy.

Forest Studies

bat⁄cave of mechanic's rags

leopards of medieval parchment
rhinoceroses of bureaucrats' cabinets

spider webs of detonation zones

moths of soldiers' lapels
millipedes of advancing Spartans

bamboo grove of Big Bird's legs

cobras of unfed babies
toads of claymation

coconuts of asylum hair

Macaws of Basquiat's palette
insects of Microsoft wingdings

rainfall of cutlery

red ants of frying pan oil
bananas of hotrod exhaust pipes

larvae of a Tiffany necklace

lake of cigarette tinfoil
lichen of psoriasis

plumage of a third-rate Elvis

mud of a Datsun's interior
beehives of winter exhalations

Open This Door

after Rachel Whiteread's "House"

The faces of strange and not strange people
nervous about looking too long at cast walls.

Inside, the children have blocky voices:
I AM HUNGRY.

They wish they could be more expansive.
All ideas are clobbered,

then they are cured like this.
Disappointed in the fear of adjacencies

and overlapping surfaces.
Every day they have an object, buy an object,

or have an object delivered.
One puts an elbow to the house,

in the ribs, and still will not buckle it.
The key bends in the lock,

the piano is crushed
in the parlor, the night-table collapses.

The only soft thing is cobweb –
brush it away before you knock.

Study of the Scent of Jasmine

It's right to read the laundry sheets
as broadsides
with nothing left to say

"not this, not this" being the sound
of crows' wings
working against sugared air – it's sickening

therefore the lungs are wings
locked in a cage.

Study of Town Dump

The collision of the life of the mind
when that mind meets its body again
doesn't it look like inevitability

that knowledge
that nothing can ever be avoided
if it could it would be called whatever

each flattened will in the trash compactor scene
Luke and Hans both at a loss in a site of loss
as if working inside the irony

museums of one or two economic views
asking the surrounding pit: is it worth it? and
you think you can hold on forever?

abandonment truly is interesting
and in need of keeping-zones like this
the output, the input, the unacceptable

Hellbox* Study

Temple roof, Godzilla~ed
then the future lies
in disassembled girders

Stalactites, clatter jut
in the mind, away,
post~power~grab: such wreckage

Theories, for the mass grave
wingless tendons
of the fallen legions

Toppled columns, of the fabled city
the half~said, last~said —
those waiting to be recalled there

Afterhours, decommissioned borders
yearning for binaries, again
lengths of rain seen from a boxcar slit

* a tray in which cast metal type
is thrown after printing.

Study of a Glass Salt Shaker

simply now, it survives

a king's last pawn
in bullet-eaten helmet

what's next, and from where?

so set against the garishness
of blood and interminable conflict

no more pain, please

and no more reductions
each body is to be embraced

each to be accepted: this is its clarity.

Study of Vacant Lot

A day with knocked-out tooth
as if space made space into a history
of unspoken hurt.

Against the probabilities of ascension,
the real is without principles:
concrete, rebar, cinder block, dirt.

There's a chance to pay attention
to the simplicity of misery –
how it flops, as if in bliss.

The Lynchian

Dear wall with stains.
Dear make/up.
Dear highway.
Dear stage with red curtains.
Dear three/legged dog.
Dear industrial sound.

I am afraid of your sound.
I am afraid of your stains.
I am afraid of your dog.
I am afraid of your make/up.
I am afraid of your curtains.
I am afraid of your highway.

Study of Steel Wool

as for these years
this is the cake of mistakes
the unspooled logic

with no more access
to past or future
only miserable constancy

as in a cuckoo clock
that explodes its doors
with a boing of wires:

the sound being
the cartoon of the loss
of wits

Pastoral Poem

when fire comes up
wheat field pities itself

and admits gold
guarantees little

and that nothingness
is always in approach

lifting a house
with no more room for denial

then turning it
until vomit comes out

it takes this
to do that

it takes that
within itself

to detox
the inhabitants

yet again it takes a turbine
to animate the bodies

then they fall like understudies
on the lawn

Study of Nail-Polished Toes
for Penny

lacquered
air-raid windows

reflecting back kerpows
of sunlight

ominous then
as Malevich's black square paintings

polish of acetone, pigment, mica,
formaldehyde, nitrocellulose

but also those at the shore who
fan their toes and pour loafer-sand in an arc

this makes an island of despair
if only we had more time

and that beach with the prints
that Crusoe finds he denies

then admits as signs of empire's ghosts
Friday is the creator and has found a way

(always knew) how to walk barefoot
against the prime meridian

and all intimations
of immortality

After John Cage

tightening the screw on the bicycle
loosens the hinge on the door
shielding the baby from sunlight
gathers clouds above the parade
polishing the red apple
scrapes the knee of the child
straightening the painting on the wall
clicks on the earthquake
restoring the moth to the night
incites the lonely to leap
completing the stone wall
collapses the bedroom floor

Nature Study

after Marcel Duchamp's "Given"

That the owl knows exactly what will occur
merely by believing in circularity

that to spin any object 360 degrees is to demonstrate
the ridiculousness of plans

that unshareable feeling of déjà vu
that particular broken neck

as if the head carried too much information
listing with a big word (destiny, perhaps)

and toppled
there it falls unevenly

into down onto within for that man
that man's thicket, splay, velvet

for the colony's vision
to look with a scavenger's eyes: hopping

from part to part
why so much hunger?

why another sale?

Study of Abstractions

one kind of order exists
and looms in the air:
a steel bridge, for instance, as a diagram
for a more rational idea of river

then another kind of disorder
discovers the importance of the spirit
in the shape of a blue flame
firing from the camper's drunk ass

i.e. an illumination
a better way to see the darkness
so there's a morality
of surrender

in a bent fork, an unlit candle,
a toy truck empty of gravel,
a clucking of rapids against rocks,
and also a cat that rolls its fluff in another cat's shit –
        why not?

After Viewing Cy Twombly's
"Fifty Days at Iliam"

in order to experience panic
the tornado stills itself

amidst the ones
who don't understand war

but do it
as bottles and rags do bombs

pushed so far that other
objects look into alternate careers, too

a shovel nosing
a stone-wheel

and a lantern flame
reaching up to the eaves

this is tenderness
according to the movements of the field

and according to the hours
that drum the moon across the sun

Tree Ring Study

And why not admit there's too much time?
Dunes of it,
and the hypnotist's spirals,
concussions of church bells – all-burying, mental.

Yet there must be peace, too.
That which teaches the pine
to stand so, record its whorls,
wait.

As if the centre could hold and
the stone's thonk in the pond
never faded, marking
one heart and its thumps.

Study of the Sound of Ripping Grass
(Handfuls)

There must be a new tyrant.
At least, the air expects changes.

Clouds, for instance, resemble
books fleeing a burning.

Music, really, for all the latest treasons
and/or an overdub for kill-lists.

Each handful emits
a panic of CB static.

What is happening? A body becoming
a beast and bursting its clothes.

Get ready.
Do something.

Peace Talks

'In the dark' describes
a crystal bowl on the pond's floor

a raven that turns out
to be a hole smashed in a stone wall
or the other way around

the carpet that's well short
of the wainscoting and wanting or not
like a salmon huffing
in between land and water

waiting for the tide
and the sand to agree again.

Study of the Eye of a Goat

A sleigh-bell without report,
pupil of the heart-rate's long dash

it knows joy levitated the wish
while the coin drowned it, that
hope sent the prayer upwards
while the clasped-hands crushed it

hence the brand of the toppled 'I'
the censor's cancellation
a knife-slit showing what's to come.

Study of Iron Frying Pan

former star, congealed
the watches of Hiroshima
& stilled the hour to the body in Dali forms

an approximation of the death of the solar
to worship useless tools still, a lady's mirror
when the world has been so scoured of light

to put a handle on a circle
in order to feel like a god
wielding an ideal form

Displacements

"the way words rally to the blanks between them and thus augment the volume of their resonance"
– Rosmarie Waldrop

The moment of displacement when the matchbook itself
catches fire. The moment when speech is lead away from
the conversation in order to move dust across the floor. The
moment when what had been drawn from a bucket appears
also to be giving form to the ladle, the hand, the arm and so
on. The moment when a school of fish scatter in order to
demonstrate shattering glass. The moment when the carpet,
for an instant, refuses to release the coffee table. The moment
when the overcoats piled on the bed assume the obscenity
of war photos. The moment after acute pain in which
a diminishment of that pain – still far off – begins. The
moment when a plant moves and the cat spikes its back.
The moment after heavy snow when bike becomes boke, car
becomes clar, and steps become splets.

Study of a Grasshopper

it has not turned out
rasp session
it has not turned out

the horizon means attack
and highway means
help me find
that burnt-off skin

harbinger, lamenter,
the chopper above
sways the grass

Sore Throat Study

the rocks of the inukshuk
clacking in wind

thus without certainty
or in want of abilities

remember the leafy branch that
goes in green and comes out bare

for the moment the well's armored with crayfish
though the breath says to and fro as before

an incubating pâté –
the relative indignity, the promise to make amends.

Moose
after Erin Mouré

A moose is a reprimand to the forest's
awe at falling leaf
as if value adheres only in stillness and the tiny.

The moose typically shits atop the glass lake.
A moose is a hair⁄do covered in candelabra⁄webs.
It's a word which stands for that solitude

found in a number of oil⁄based
contexts: black pond, summer field,
approaching storm.

In practice, it is usually an organism which,
by its movements,
resembles three adults: head, back, and asshole.

In a moose world, snow collects
on top of the long head
in order to cool the heat of the brain.

Nest Study

a scribble with dimension
and redirections

which the bird knows
and doesn't

collecting line after line
of weaves to make a bowl

so that air is invited
and lost all at once

and 'in and out' give up
in the gathering

Mongrel Study

Inside the mottled muppet
is a puppeteer, also famished.

A village rock that stood up
and carried the hide away with it.

Or one moss wall, in ruins
so precarious the wind sways it

until the possibility arrives
that his (why must it be his?) coat

conceals a cave door that flaps open
onto The Hall of Bulls at Lascaux.

Water

after Federico Garcia Lorca

The water lifts
in a green vest.

The water releases the body
as a cub

falling through cedar
branches.

The water is crazy.
Sick of censure, sick of praise.

Study of Butterflies
after Vladimir Nabokov

the wobbling flight path
anticipates chloroform

'summer afternoon' being line one
of the haiku

that writes
their death amongst cornflowers

yet they don't die, really
rather enter into a field

or move atop it
as if an image over a lake

and so to be carried
as a thought within a man

a man being a book
that needs words and words

being that which once lived
with no need for referents.

Pantoum for Standard Keyboard

There's a tilde of gull.
There's an exclamation mark of baseball bat!
There's an at-symbol of vortex.
There's a number sign of gauze.

There's an exclamation of baseball bat!
There's a dollar sign of python and prey.
There's a number sign of gauze.
There's a percent sign of a Picasso face.

There's a dollar sign of python and prey.
There's a circumflex of the diver's back.
There's a percent sign of a Picasso face.
There's an ampersand of Ingres.

There's a circumflex of the diver's back.
There's an asterisk of desert sun.
There's an ampersand of Ingres.
There's a left parenthesis of Ubu's gut.

There's an asterisk of desert sun.
There's a right parenthesis of Hitchcock's jowl.
There's a left parenthesis of Ubu's gut.
There's an underscore of the cellar step.

There's a right parenthesis of Hitchcock's jowl.
There a plus sign of the rifle's scope.

There's an underscore of the cellar step.
There's a tilde of gull.

Sewer Grate Study

Fletches for proof that it is a hurtling object.
And the flood is a cause for celebration.

Each grate is a station
of this∕and∕that: a cross

between filter/prison and
archive/thief's cave.

One always walks over shipwrecks.
This is grace. To start again. To reject

plenitude and embrace grief.
Loss is predictable: necklaces

slip from the neck because objects believe
in transformation.

To substantiate this,
it grew gills.

Poem for the Death of a Draughtsman
(Käthe Kollwitz)

Charcoal works for fire still,
grinds itself into the paper

as if hoping for re-ignition.
This won't happen.

But what about the twinning
of the smoke, sketched

to resemble the landscape
smoldering outside?

How potato field and plough
get transferred – all rendered

within a whiff of burn?
These two humans held in harness

are dumb,
made so by modern contexts.

Which permit little holding
and more and more of release

as part of the scene depends
on the elements of the body

that are given up,
blown off the field,

off the table, off the drawing paper,
and into the air.

Wheat Study

it shakes a rattler's tail
(this is known) and
the braid duplicates the scuttle⁄print
across the beach in order
to get to first embraces, i.e. one body
finding another (complete)

there's a horizon created by
sky and land – there's difference
and no difference, separation
and no separation
the wheat stretches in order to
plait them together.

Study for the Slowness of Underwater Hair

what exists is gentle
to reach but never to gather all that much

to shake, as they say, violently
only to draw attention to more silence

what's the reward for mystery?
who's got a story about survival?

as when the red handkerchief
waves at the bull

the billowing gives form
to what stillness could be or was up until then

to lift as horses' manes lift
patient when galloping over a hill

the grass on the ridge,
collective pulse and sway

there is no strategy there,
no strictures, no fear.

Sheep Study

On this hill a gathering of brains
and just enough language
left within them
to say yeah

drawn out, like a question:
what is stupid? what's lament?
call it torpor, lostness, indifference
they have needs but have forgotten them

therefore they assemble and wait
to impersonate thought bubbles
in want of text — the landscape
may or may not bring ideas

the wind hustles them
and the money-in-a-jar river
offers one sentence
that does not end

they look out at the highway:
tell us what we are.

Apollinaire's Speech to the War Medic

and what about this other world
where what is asked to stay gentle, stays

and all forks, shovels, and pistols
are wrapped in gauze

is it really safe?
if so, who lives there?

our world is the scene
in which the legs stick out of the malmsey butt

it's just a matter of time – what? –
to signify or not

that the tendency of truth
is to lie in exceptions

one day the bullet will grow its own skull
and reside inside it

then it will have no need for us

Blood Study

That's the pestle, grinding raspberries for the passion;
the lopped leg of the rabbit and the neck of the chicken,
dripping into the offering bowl; whenever it acquires
sentience, it runs; shouldn't it? that mouth, who says its
lipstick is red, is actually leaking information; desire flies
out, too, as in the Shogun's sprayed wall in *Ran*; hungry and
cold at this very moment, then later pushing mercury up its
glass tunnel; to the metropolitan police, the outlines on the
linoleum are more telling than the knives – there is some
truth to absence, then; the way Bruce tasted his own loss and
went hysterical, as if every escape of it could be entitled 'too
much reality;' as if the rose garden might, with a fall of the
sun, be the killing floor.

Light & Char

"The true path is along a rope, not a rope suspended way up in the air, but rather only just over the ground. It seems more like a tripwire than a tightrope."

— Franz Kafka

Preamble

As if the sidewalk believed, with enough foot traffic, it might be polished into a mirror; seeing the sun above and atop and down below: the cosmos (woah) may be addressed as "less and all." As if Osip Mandelstam returned (within it) to say, "Psst. The sun's shining and yet no one should expect happiness ..." Come again? The censor and the black marker's eclipse. As if the candle flame was a gap in the stage-curtain or as if the darkness was two hands trying to hold a bird: the page ignites for light and for char.

On Difference (Knots)

Study, Executioner, the halyard, reef, bowline, sheep shank, and the succession of slips. This impersonation of nothings (droop and wilt and limp) gets tautened into the finality – a togethered snapping-to. Amazing or ehn [shrug]. Then? To unite, like this. And when the mother saws the rope from the son's neck then knife, neck, and rope are also past, present, and future. According to the blood, none of these objects are unique. Once the knife breathed in and out, the rope cut itself, and the throat tied its own noose.

On Safety (Bricks)

Fuck it. The smartest pig resolves to brick⁄up the doorway,
damn the windows, and stuff the chimney with mortar.
Goodbye, remarkable tree: the ten⁄hut of the trunk, the
leaves' sustained fireworks. So long, apple rotating just so
into the sunlight. It's usually up to the moon (farewell) to
spike the wolf's fur while it sleeps. That's desire, too, isn't it?
… any thrill – good or bad! – from elsewhere? Well, adios
bear shit versus lilac perfume. No more goosebumps, then.
The trowel labours against tensions and harmonies – until
the bricks make a crypt of unreadable books.

On Secrets (Paper)

According to the radio, the song is "O wife, you blank
thing." For instance, in transfering vegetables (from
colander to plate) she is said to be of routine and diurnal.
Yet on the cutting board, couldn't the chopped potatoes be
skulls? In that candle-lit story, when everyone else sleeps,
the monk rises up again and works. Mercy, for the cold air;
mercy, for the pushed-out breath that shapes itself into...yes?
a secret verb? Only in setting it down – setting it down –
does the house begin to reappear around the page: Kenmore
vaccuum, cereal bowl, keys, grocery list.

On Denial (Junebug)

Hunkered gestapo, Tollund toenail – waiting for one word
to activate the big transformation: bloom it out of char and
back into fire again. Only some chants are permissible,
contingent on the experience of the town cryer. Like the
bellow: run. The news is usually 'don't tell us.' The news
is 'let pleasure reign.' In two fields separated by a concrete
wall, the body that splits in half is highly moral but
practically screwed. And this is a machine, muttering with
that classified information. It hurtles down and it never
resolves – a burnt satellite, sizzling in the grass.

On Death (Paint)

The flies have the nature of asterisks spinning in turpentine.
Check the footer: a paragraph about time, the skin as
sieve – explicated (to death, again) into method. Where
is the sin in this? Well, right here. Art needs... art doesn't
care, actually. There, the entire supply of linen, hung
on the line, and worked on with paint until the panel is
indistinguishable from the forest. Reserved horizon, just
to make an enigma for game – that is, will the deer run
differently inside the canvas? This way→ to want a thing,
this way→ to see the brush as tongue and the poison in the
tongue, too.

On Memory (Boxes)

To forget the purpose of either recollection or amnesia,
then the box exists. The magician demonstrates the box's
liberality. Nearly a magazine-cut-out of a tropical bird (on
a trapeze-perch and lowered inside), the lovely assistant
asks the audience, "Is memory modern? Is symbol old-
fashioned?" Within and without – else how would the
illusion carry? – the victim must revert to total emptiness in
order to really hide. Ta da, for instance, as the sound of two
steps towards loss. They find, in the absence, either the proof
of memory or of its mechanical malfunction.

On Mischief (Masks)

If it deepens, it's mise en abyme; as when spreading the
deck of cards diagonally across the table creates Muybridge
photographs. If the gag keeps going then 'identity' is proved
false in *Scooby Doo*. The cellar as an order of darkness;
the cedar chest in the cellar as a deeper order of darkness.
Then the cut-out eyes equal 'and so on.' As if too true to be
suffered, the mask is ripped off and dashed to the ground.
There it is. So in the environment of the newspaper cartoon,
it's traditional to mount human heads above the mantle
while, below, the deer sip sherry and read the funnies.

On Peace (Barrows)

All predicates rammed into a memorial, the burial hump of
death-bed speech. This mute embankment, and Euripides'
(for instance) entire cast within. When it's resolved the
mound opens its mouth... as a reptile's eyelid... and a –
without the eternity gulp? well, except to the mouth-that-
speaks being conjoined to the mouth-that-devours. Fine,
without any need, any -ings at all: just this completion: tail
into throat. Wonderful. Goody. It agrees with the clarities of
the great plains as well as with the opacities of the warrior's
gouge. No, it neither agrees nor disagrees.

On Justice (Rooms)

Bring instead, to Room 101, all the assholes. Consider last week's event: the kitchen and the milk, being identical, the pitcher poured an absence into the glass while the shadow couldn't stick. Louise's report arrives: "As to the question of redress, all of us grew fat on Papa's body." A man complained. Kathy's report, too: "The goblin fucked me and then I fucked the goblin." The cops can't see crockery-as-archive or the egg shells as rehearsals for coups d'etat. And Nadezhda's whisper is the last one in the telephone game: "It was more important, for the future, that I became a book."

On Pain (Funerals)
for Georgie and Don Summerhayes

Cross-section of the ant farm: the Franklin Gothic in a
book set by a drunkard. It reads, uh, "What tree does the
bloody fall from today?" Is that right? Out of a maple and
into a maple. Scooped, conciliatory as a canoe: use me,
because this coffin travels... Or, clicking off the Orpheus
radio: those who are expecting to be floating on gusts of
supremely good karma consider that even the darkest of
poems will never save the corpse from the rot of light and
air. So how does this work again: look up... stars tighten
into fists – and they too can't hold on.

On Vitality (Skyscrapers)

If only one might see that they do not "shoot up into the air" but rather "grow down from clouds." Notice how they work for calm but long for danger: calling it hail yet casting dice in the shape of skulls too; so where's the vitality in such clatter: in the spaces that surround? the wind? the glass? all the in-betweens? At whatever level, they entreat one's 'me' to step out of the emergency exit into freefall. Now is realism, surrealism, conceptualism, and "my rock video" the all-at-once condition. Swoosh, says the nothingness and it says it like ho-hum.

On Linearity (Bridges)

But 'trouble' is only a problem outside of art and – you
know it – ain't nothing outside of beauty. Then myths
appear: such as breath⁄fog on the vanity mirror. In it,
eventually, five or six straight lines, one circle and an upside
down U to make an existentialist. So it's Mr. Cyncial today.
That which lives in a cloud, a cyclone, and the everyday
swirl: what one walks through... what one rolls in, Pigpen.
Hey, there's no need for threshold spanners – there's no
chasms, and there's nothing underneath to dread!

On Beauty (Worms)

Against the solidities of the elegant (a plate on a wall; dog's
claw; Hepworth sculpture); how does so much get eaten?
In the name of darkness? For the sake of reckoning? Nope,
no. It's worms doing the grotesque revolt of nails: entropic
history: slackening refusal; insideouting of certainties:
everything that was pinned is unhinged as an excretion;
crash: that's the Bedroom at Arles canvas sliding down the
wall; crashsplash, too: there goes Fallingwater drooping into
the water; every absolute called back to the banal; to be, say,
this empty and to be programmed only for more.

On Wounds (Sewing)

As when, after stabbing and gouging the wall, one eye on
this side meets one eye on that side. As in, what do you
have? Whadda u got? Then, stagger back, it's a kerpow in
the archive: opening an antique book onto a pressed bat: "I
got this jagged hole that yearns from all sides." Or "my sister
put this shit here" or "don't ask me, ask it" or just "bandage,
please." It's true that the grass will sometimes split apart
to honour the otherworldliness of the daydreamer. In that
yawning, just before the descent, this is what "all people"
means.

Acknowledgements

Thank you to the kind editors of *McSweeney's Internet Tendency, Nthposition,* CBC's *Daybreak, Ryga,* Bookthug, and Greenboathouse Press who published/broadcasted some of these poems in earlier forms. Deep thank yous of support are also due to Maricia Barschelaby, derek beaulieu, Mike Boulter, Don Coles, Mr. Craxie, Beks Croker, Anne Fleming, Nancy Holmes, Paul Hong, Big Dave Jefferess, Sasha Johnston, Sean Johnston, Sharon Josephson, Matt Kavanagh, John Lent, Craig McLuckie, Jay MillAr, David Nault, Paola Poletto, Sina Queyras, Alya Ramadan, Jordan Scott, Stu, Sharon Thesen, and Marilyn & David Werry. And yawping thank yous to my two main back-getters kevin mcpherson eckhoff and Jason Dewinetz. Hey, Rae Kennedy and Marlo Edwards, thank you to you both, too. And, finally, thank you to NFP – to whom this book is dedicated.

About the Author

Jake Kennedy was born in the tobacco-land of Woodstock, Ontario and grew up in the big-box-land of Mississauga, Ontario. Now Jake lives and works happily in the Okanagan. Some of Jake's writing has appeared in *McSweeney's Internet Tendency, Pissing Ice: New Canadian Poets, Drunken Boat, Kiss Machine*, and *The Diagram*. His BookThug chapbook entitled *Hazard* won the 2007 bpnichol Chapbook Award. Jake also helped edit, with his artist friend Paola Poletto, *Boredom Fighters: A Graphic Poem Anthology* in 2008. Most recently, Jake received the Robert Kroetsch Award for Innovative Poetry for *The Lateral.* He is working currently on an entirely made-up (but reverent) biography of New York poet-architect Madeline Gins. Jake is also co-compiling, with his great friend kevin mcpherson eckhoff, *Death Valley: a Collaborative Community Novel.*

Colophon

Manufactured in an edition of 500 copies in the
spring of 2011 by BookThug. Distributed in Canada
by the Literary Press Group WWW.LPG.CA.
Distributed in the United States by Small Press
Distribution WWW.SPDBOOKS.ORG.
Shop on-line at WWW.BOOKTHUG.CA.

BOOK
PRODUCTION
WAR ECONOMY
STANDARD

Type + design by Jay MillAr
Cover image by David Nault
"Skullture" by kevin mcpherson eckhoff